The
LITTLE BOOK OF
STUDENT FOOD

Alastair Williams

summersdale

THE LITTLE BOOK OF STUDENT FOOD

This revised edition copyright © Summersdale Publishers Ltd, 2019

Previously published as *Student Grub* in 2013

An Hachette UK Company
www.hachette.co.uk

Summersdale Publishers Ltd
Part of Octopus Publishing Group Limited
Carmelite House
50 Victoria Embankment
LONDON
EC4Y 0DZ
UK

www.summersdale.com

Printed and bound in Poland

ISBN: 978-1-78783-024-0

Substantial discounts on bulk quantities of Summersdale books are available to corporations, professional associations and other organisations. For details contact general enquiries: telephone: +44 (0) 1243 771107 or email: enquiries@summersdale.com.

Contents

Introduction

Welcome to *The Little Book of Student Food*! As the title suggests, this is meant to be an affordable, pocket-sized guide rather than a costly, clunky compendium. And it's for students of all abilities. If you've never made anything more adventurous than toast, this book will start you off on the road to culinary glory. But if you're already quite comfortable in the kitchen, there are plenty of exciting recipes from around the world to develop your repertoire.

The key factors for student cookery are obviously cost, time and taste, which is why these recipes can be whipped up cheaply and quickly without compromising on flavour. And once you've got them mastered, you can experiment by using different ingredients.

Student life can be fast-paced and chaotic, of course, but learning how to feed yourself well is one of the best things you can do for your health, happiness and academic success. You're bound to make mistakes along the way, but that's all part of the fun. Enjoy the journey, try new things and make these recipes your own.

A NOTE FOR VEGETARIANS AND VEGANS

A good number of the recipes in this book are already vegetarian or vegan-friendly, but most of the others can be adapted for those who prefer not to eat meat or any animal products.

Non-dairy alternatives for milk, cream, butter and cheese are now widely available in most supermarkets, and a large variety of plant-based "meats" are also out there. Use the same measurements given in the recipes, but always feel free to adapt things as you see fit.

Eggs are used in some of the baking recipes to bind the ingredients, but apple purée is a great alternative. Batches can be frozen into ice-cube trays in advance – assume one defrosted cube (or 1 tablespoon) is roughly equivalent to one egg.

THE BASICS

WHAT YOU NEED

The chances are that your student kitchen, as well as being a health liability, will lack the modern appliances that a lot of family kitchens have. The idea of attempting a meal without fancy gadgets may seem daunting, but it can be done. Many student kitchens will not even have a set of scales, so many of the measurements given use spoons (tablespoons, teaspoons) and grams (which you can convert into spoons or cups – see the conversion chart on page 11).

You may also need some patience. Many of the recipes are super quick and simple, but when attempting something more adventurous it is essential not to give up. Some people will find cooking very easy, but it's not everyone's strong suit, and some of us need a little more perseverance and composure. Cooking disasters are all part of the fun, though, and practice makes perfect.

COMMON SENSE

The recipes in this book are designed with simplicity in mind, both in terms of the implements and skills required. Cooking times and temperatures are approximate because cooking is often an intuitive process and no number of instructions can replace common sense and initiative.

Before you try any recipe, read it all the way through first to make sure you have all the right ingredients and equipment you need. You'll also need to make sure you have enough time to carry out all the steps. And remember to preheat your oven to the correct temperature before you put anything in it.

HEALTH AND SAFETY

If you are in a large shared house or halls of residence, the kitchen may have to cater to the needs of many people, and it is quite easy when sharing a small kitchen for it to become unhygienic. It's a good idea in these situations to organize some sort of rota for cooking and cleaning. If one or two people cook each night for everyone it avoids the hassle that would occur if everybody in the house waited to use the cooker for themselves. It also means that you will only be cooking perhaps once or twice a week – win-win.

Once you have established that your cooking environment is clean and hygienic, pay special attention to these instructions for food storage.

- **All perishable foodstuffs will have a best-before date printed on their packaging, and clear instructions on how long they can languish in your fridge before they need to be eaten or disposed of (use-by date). This is especially important when it comes to meat and dairy products.**

- Frozen foods need to be kept hard frozen until you start cooking them.

- If food is defrosted it must be cooked and cooled before refreezing.

- Warm food should not be placed directly into a fridge – wait for it to cool down first.

- When food is left out on the countertop for more than a couple of hours, it can develop harmful bacteria – so don't eat it!

CONVERSIONS AND MEASUREMENTS

The recipes in this book are typically given in metric measurements, but many small amounts are measured in spoons or cups (1 cup is roughly equal to 16 tablespoons or 150 g of flour).

tbsp = tablespoon (1 tbsp equals roughly 15 ml or 0.6 fl. oz)
tsp = teaspoon (1 tsp equals roughly 5 ml or 0.2 fl. oz)

All spoon measures refer to level spoons, not heaped. Spoon measures can also be substituted for grams with certain ingredients, which is handy for those without a set of kitchen scales. Obviously the weights of all ingredients will vary, but here are some rough measures:

1 tbsp ≈ 25 g (1 oz) of... syrup, jam, honey
2 tbsp ≈ 25 g (1 oz) of... butter, sugar
3 tbsp ≈ 25 g (1 oz) of... cornflour, cocoa, custard, flour
4 tbsp ≈ 25 g (1 oz) of... grated cheese, porridge oats

If you don't want to use metric measurements, and you don't have a smartphone to do the conversions for you, here are some basic tables:

25 g ≈ 1 oz	15 ml ≈ 0.5 fl. oz
60 g ≈ 2 oz	30 ml ≈ 1 fl. oz
85 g ≈ 3 oz	75 ml ≈ 2.5 fl. oz
115 g ≈ 4 oz	120 ml ≈ 4 fl. oz
255 g ≈ 9 oz	270 ml ≈ 9 fl. oz

Where given in this book, oven temperatures are presented in Celsius, Fahrenheit and gas mark, but as a rule of thumb for cooking purposes Celsius is roughly half the Fahrenheit temperature. Set fan-assisted ovens 25°C (approximately 50°F) lower than others and reduce the time spent cooking by 10 minutes for every hour of cooking time.

GLOSSARY OF COOKING TERMS

Baste – To spoon fat or oil over food to keep it moist. Usually done to a joint of meat while it is in the oven.

Beat – This is the mixing of ingredients using a wooden spoon, a fork or a whisk.

Chop – To cut into small pieces.

Cream – To mix fat with another ingredient like sugar until it becomes creamy.

Dice – To cut into small cubes.

Grate – A grater can produce coarse or fine shavings of food, such as cheese or vegetables.

Knead – To use your knuckles to smooth dough out, the idea being to get a smooth texture.

Marinade – A combination of juices, spices and oils in which meat is soaked to enhance the flavour.

Parboil – This is the partial boiling of something. The cooking of the food will then normally be finished off by another method, e.g. roasting potatoes.

Peel – To remove the skin or the outer layer of a vegetable.

Rub in – To rub flour and fat together between your fingertips until they resemble breadcrumbs.

Simmer – To cook just below the boiling point, so that only an occasional bubble appears on the surface.

Steam – One of the healthiest ways to prepare vegetables, while ensuring they keep their crunch. Steamers are widely and cheaply available in different styles, or you can use a makeshift one by placing the veg in a colander and resting above a pan of boiling water, with a lid on top.

Stir-fry – To fry quickly while stirring regularly in a hot pan or wok. Healthier than traditional frying as it uses less oil.

Top and tail – To cut off the drier, knobbly ends of vegetables such as carrots, leeks, sweet potatoes, etc.

Healthy Eating

Normally, when living at home and eating three square meals a day (presumably including plenty of vegetables and fruit), you will receive all the vitamins and minerals needed to stay healthy. All this can change when you go away to study. Eating at irregular times can become the norm as you juggle studying with an active social life.

If you want to stay healthy you must eat a balanced diet. There are certain things that are essential to achieving this. Let's take a quick look at them.

CARBOHYDRATES

These are the main providers of energy. They also happen to be the cheapest types of food and can be found in things like potatoes, bread, rice and pasta. Although these foods are always available in ample supply, be mindful of your intake, because an excess of carbohydrates can lead to obesity.

FATS

These also provide energy for the body, but they take longer to digest than carbohydrates. This means they are useful for storing energy. There are two main types of fats: saturated and unsaturated. Excessive saturated fat can lead to heart disease, diabetes and high blood pressure, and should only be consumed in moderation – it is present in products like butter, margarine, milk, cheese and red meat. Unsaturated fat is good for you, helping the body absorb nutrients and providing energy – it's found in avocados, nuts, lean meat (such as skinless chicken or turkey), olives and fish.

PROTEINS

The word "protein" has a Greek origin and means "of first importance", which is exactly what proteins are. They're necessary for bodily development and repairs to damaged cells. You find them in fish, lean meat, vegetables, grains, beans, nuts, seeds, soy products, milk, cheese and eggs.

VITAMINS

This is one area where many students fail to supply the correct amounts vital to keeping the body in perfect running order. The following is a list of the most essential vitamins and their sources:

- **Vitamin A** – present in dairy products like cheese, eggs and milk, and in green vegetables, fish and liver.

- **Vitamin B** – made up of more than ten different vitamins. They are found in wholegrain cereals, liver, yeast, lean meat, beans, peas and nuts.

- **Vitamin C** – lack of vitamin C results in scurvy, a common problem on naval ships way back in history, but you're still at risk today if you don't eat the right foods. The main source of the vitamin is citrus fruits like lemons and oranges, and blackcurrants and fresh vegetables. Vitamin C is great for the immune system and helps to protect against the common cold.

- **Vitamin D** – essential for the absorption of calcium, a deficiency of which can lead to rickets in children, which means the bones are weak. In adults it can result in bow legs. The main way our bodies get vitamin D is through exposure to sunlight, but this can be in pretty short supply sometimes – especially if you are holed up in a lecture theatre or the library. Luckily the vitamin can also be found in milk, butter, cheese, fish and liver, but a daily supplement of 10 mg will also do the job.

- **Vitamin E** – this is a vitamin that does not usually pose a deficiency problem. It is found in avocados, tomatoes, spinach, watercress, blackberries, mangoes, nuts, wholegrains, olive oil, mackerel and salmon.

- **Vitamin K** – this is found in green vegetables and wholegrain cereals. It is important in helping your blood to clot.

ROUGHAGE (AKA DIETARY FIBRE)

This is vital if you want to have a healthily functioning digestive system and avoid constipation. High-fibre cereals and fruit and vegetables provide good sources of roughage.

WATER

Your body requires up to 3 litres (100 fl. oz) a day to function, so this is a reminder.

MINERALS

There are three main minerals which are important for health: iron, calcium and iodine. Other minerals such as phosphates, potassium, magnesium and sodium are generally in good supply in most people's diets.

- **Iron** – this is vital for the formation of red blood cells. If a person has a deficiency of iron it can lead to anaemia. Ensuring a high iron intake is not as simple as eating a bag of nails, however. Far better to eat liver, which is slightly more palatable, and is an excellent source of iron, as are other meats, dried herbs, seeds and dark green leafy vegetables.

- **Calcium** – this mineral is important for strong bones and teeth. It is found in dairy products like milk, butter and cheese, tofu and soy products and green leafy vegetables.

- **Iodine** – although important in the production of thyroid hormones, iodine is not needed in the same quantities as calcium or iron. Fish, milk, yogurt and seaweed are good sources of iodine.

The Store Cupboard

You never want to be in the middle of cooking when you discover that you're lacking a crucial ingredient. Here's a list of suggestions to keep always at the ready.

CANS

Apart from the obligatory cans of alcoholic refreshment, canned food is always useful for its longevity. Examples include:

Baked beans | chickpeas | coconut milk | kidney beans | lentils | ravioli | soups | sweetcorn | tomatoes | tuna | tinned fruit

OILS

If you store them away from heat and light, they will keep for ages. Here are the classics:

Olive oil | sunflower oil | vegetable oil

DRIED FRUITS

If you don't use them in recipes, they are also perfect for healthy snacking:

Apricots | banana chips | dates | sultanas, currants and raisins

FLOUR

There are so many varieties of flour available nowadays, but here are some basics:

Plain | wholemeal | self-raising | buckwheat

NUTS AND SEEDS

Keep unsalted versions of the following at the ready for adding to recipes or for a nutritious snack:

Almonds | cashews | walnuts | peanuts | pumpkin seeds | sunflower seeds

CARBS

These are starchy staples that should form part of any balanced diet (in moderation):

Pasta | rice | noodles | couscous | quinoa

SUGAR

Here are the four basics:

Granulated | caster | icing | brown

SPICES, HERBS AND SEASONINGS

Given moderate use, these can transform a plain-tasting meal into something special. Just remember the amounts used have to be carefully controlled, the idea being to enhance the flavour of the food, not to annihilate your taste buds.

When a recipe includes "salt and pepper" it generally means a pinch of each, but it is up to the individual to season according to taste. One of the most essential items in a kitchen should be a pepper mill. Freshly ground pepper tastes so much better than the stuff that is pre-ground, so try to get hold of one. Here are the most commonly used spices, herbs and seasonings:

- **Basil**
- **Bay leaves**
- **Black pepper**
- **Capers**
- **Caraway seeds**

- **Cayenne pepper**
- **Chillies**
- **Chilli powder**
- **Chives**
- **Cinnamon**

- Cloves
- Curry powder
- Garam masala
- Garlic
- Lemon juice
- Mace
- Marjoram
- Mint
- Mustard (French or English)
- Nutmeg
- Oregano
- Paprika pepper
- Parsley
- Rosemary
- Sage
- Salt
- Soy sauce
- Sweet and sour sauce
- Tabasco sauce
- Thyme
- Vinegar (cider, malt or wine)
- Worcestershire sauce

SOUPS AND STARTERS

Garlic Bread

This classic student recipe is a great addition to spaghetti bolognese.

INGREDIENTS

150 g of butter
2 cloves of garlic
1 stick of French bread

Put the butter in a small mixing bowl. It helps if the butter is soft. Peel and finely chop the garlic and add to the butter, mixing well with a fork. Slice the French stick at 4-cm (1.5-inch) intervals, without actually severing it, and spread some of the butter on both sides of each slit. Then close up the gaps and wrap the loaf in foil. Place in the oven and cook for 15 to 20 minutes at Gas Mark 5 (190°C, 375°F).

Carrot and Ginger Soup

This is one of the tastiest soups around – the ginger gives it a delicious flavour that never fails to impress.

Serves 4

INGREDIENTS

500 g of carrots
1 potato
1 piece of fresh root ginger
  (approx. 4 cm or 1.5 in. long)
1 litre of water
2 tbsp of single cream (optional)
Salt
Pepper

Peel and chop the carrots, potato and ginger (keep the pieces of ginger large enough that you can remove them later – into quarters should do it).

Place the carrots, potato and ginger in a pan and cover with the water. Bring to the boil and then simmer for 20 minutes. Remove from the heat and take out the ginger.

Transfer the ingredients into a blender and blend until a smooth consistency is achieved. Season according to taste and stir in the cream, if desired.

TOP TIP

Whenever a recipe tells you to simmer, make sure there are only one or two bubbles coming up every few seconds. Any more than this and you need to turn the heat down.

Tomato Soup

Hearty and warming, this soup always makes you feel good.

Serves 4

INGREDIENTS

1 kg of tinned tomatoes
1 tbsp of olive oil
1 onion
2 tsp tomato purée
25 g of flour
500 ml of vegetable stock
1 bay leaf
Salt
Pepper

Heat the oil in a large saucepan. Peel and finely chop the onion and add to the pan, along with the tomatoes, purée and flour, and fry gently in the oil for about 10 minutes.

Add the stock and the bay leaf, bring to the boil, then simmer for 40 minutes. Remove the bay leaf and season.

Give the soup a blitz with a handheld blender if you have one, or a normal blender if you don't.

Vegetable Soup

There are no limits to what vegetables you can use –
these are just a guideline.

Serves 4

INGREDIENTS

2 tbsp of olive oil

1 onion

1 leek

2 cabbage leaves

1 courgette

1 carrot

1 litre of vegetable stock

1 bay leaf

Salt

Pepper

Heat the oil in a large saucepan, then peel and chop the
onion and fry for about 5 minutes or until it has softened.
Meanwhile, finely slice the leek, cabbage, courgette
and carrot and add these to the pan. Fry for a further
10 minutes. Add the stock, bay leaf and seasoning, bring
to the boil, then simmer for 30 minutes. Remove the bay
leaf before serving. If you want a smoother-tasting soup,
blend before serving.

MAINS AND SALADS

Cottage Pie

This simple and traditional dish has stood the test of time because it's so comforting and delicious – and easy to make.

Serves 3 to 4

INGREDIENTS

2 tbsp of olive oil

1 onion

1 clove of garlic

500 g of minced beef

1 tin of chopped tomatoes

1 tbsp of tomato purée

1 tsp of mixed herbs

Salt

Pepper

5 medium potatoes, peeled

Butter

Milk

Peel and finely chop the onion and garlic clove. Heat the oil in a largish saucepan, add the onion and garlic, and fry for 3 to 4 minutes on a high heat until golden. Add the meat and cook for another 10 minutes, then add the other ingredients, except for the potatoes, butter and milk, and simmer for 15 minutes.

While this is simmering, boil the potatoes in a separate pan (test them with a knife – the knife should pass through the potatoes easily), remove them from the water, then mash them with a knob of butter and a bit of milk. Put the meat in an ovenproof dish and cover with the mashed potato, then place under the grill until the potato browns.

Toad in the Hole

A classic British dish with a name guaranteed to amuse or confuse your friends from overseas.

Serves 4

INGREDIENTS

100 g of flour
Salt
1 egg
250 ml of milk
500 g of sausages (pork or vegetarian)
4 tbsp of vegetable oil

Mix the flour with a pinch of salt, then make a well in the flour and break the egg into it. Add first a little milk to give a smooth texture, then pour in the rest of the milk and beat for a minute or so to form a batter.

Put the sausages in a baking tin with the oil and bake for 10 minutes at Gas Mark 7 (220°C, 425°F).

Then add the batter and cook for a further 25 minutes or until the batter has risen and is browned.

Pork and Cider Casserole

Pork and apple has always been a classic culinary pairing and this dish is a great winter warmer.

Serves 4

INGREDIENTS

2 tbsp of olive oil

1 large onion

2 cloves of garlic

1 green pepper

4 pork chops

1 tin of chopped tomatoes

1 tbsp of tomato purée

2 tsp of mixed herbs

1 courgette

Salt

Pepper

500 ml of dry cider

1 cup of macaroni

½ cup of frozen peas

Peel and chop the onion and garlic, and deseed and chop the green pepper. Heat the oil in a large casserole dish, add the onion, garlic and green pepper, and fry for about 5 minutes. Then add the pork chops and fry on both sides for a couple of minutes. Add the tomatoes, purée, herbs, sliced courgette, seasoning and cider, then bring to the boil.

Simmer for about 40 minutes, adding the macaroni about 10 minutes before serving and the peas about 5 minutes later. Check to see if the macaroni is cooked before serving – if it's still crunchy it needs a little longer.

Meatballs

Meatballs are so versatile, and make a great accompaniment to spaghetti, rice, noodles or even mashed potato. Replace the beef with a plant-based alternative if you're vegetarian or vegan.

Serves 4

INGREDIENTS

3 slices of bread

1 onion

1 tbsp of parsley

500 g of minced beef

1 tsp of chilli powder

1 tsp of smooth French mustard

1 egg, beaten

Salt

Pepper

2 tbsp of olive oil

Remove the crusts from the bread, then tear into minuscule pieces. Those with a blender can give them a whizz for a few seconds.

Peel and chop the onion, and chop the parsley. Mix together with the breadcrumbs and add the mince, chilli powder, mustard, egg and seasoning together and mould into balls.

Heat the oil in a frying pan and fry the balls evenly for about 10 to 15 minutes, turning regularly. Don't make the balls too big or they will not cook in the middle.

Roast Dinners

The traditional Sunday roast is still as popular as ever, and the options for adding your own unique twist to this classic meal are endless. Before roasting any meat you can stuff the joint with anything from the traditional stuffing (either from a packet or home-made) to fruit, herbs, spices or vegetables – or even another type of meat! Those sharing a house will find it is good to make the effort to share a roast, as it makes a pleasant change from all the rushed meals that are grabbed between lectures during the rest of the week.

Remember that when using the oven, it should be switched on 20 minutes before the joint is put in to heat it up to the correct temperature.

ROAST BEEF

Before throwing away the packaging for your joint, note how much it weighs. Allow 20 minutes cooking time per 500 g, plus 20 minutes on top, all at Gas Mark 7 (220°C, 425°F). This will allow for cooking the meat "English style", i.e. with not too much blood seeping out. If you prefer it "rare", cook for about 15 minutes less.

Put the joint in a roasting tin and pour 125 ml of vegetable oil over the top and the sides. Season heavily with salt and pepper and any herbs of your choice, and stick in the oven.

The joint must be "basted" – that means spooning the oil in the tin over the top of the meat to stop it from drying out. Do this two or three times during cooking.

When the meat is cooked, carve the joint and serve with steamed vegetables and roast potatoes. Gravy can be made from the juices in the roasting tin by adding a small amount of flour and stirring over a medium heat to thicken, then bulking up with beef stock.

ROAST PORK

This must be cooked for a little longer than beef, as it is essential that pork is well cooked. Prepare in the same method as the beef but cook for 25 minutes per 500 g, plus 25 minutes over, on the same oven setting. Baste the joint every 20 minutes. If you like garlic, try sticking whole cloves in the joint before cooking.

ROAST LAMB

Lamb can be quite expensive but has a wonderful flavour that makes it worth splashing out on occasionally. Prepare in the same method as the beef and cook for 20 minutes per 500 g and 20 minutes extra on the same oven setting. Baste every 20 minutes. Add some sprigs of rosemary for extra flavour.

ROAST CHICKEN

It is important not to overcook chicken as it loses all its flavour and is harder to carve, yet it is imperative that the meat is fully cooked through. You can check by sticking a skewer or fork into the bird, and if the juices run clear, it's good to eat. Place the chicken in a baking tin with 125 ml of oil and season with plenty of black pepper. Bake for 15 to 20 minutes per pound plus 20 minutes extra at Gas Mark 6 (200°C, 400°F).

Basic Tomato Pasta

Does what it says on the tin: simple but satisfying.

Serves 3 to 4

INGREDIENTS

1 large onion
2 cloves of garlic
2 tbsp of olive oil
1 tin of chopped tomatoes
1 tbsp of tomato purée
6 fresh basil leaves or 1 tsp of dried oregano
Salt
Pepper
200 g of pasta of your choice

Peel and chop the onion and garlic. Heat the oil in a saucepan, then add the onion and garlic and fry gently for 3 to 4 minutes. When these have softened, add the tomatoes, purée, herbs, salt and pepper. Cook for another 20 minutes until they have been reduced.

Meanwhile, cook the pasta according to packet instructions and, when cooked, drain and stir together with the sauce.

To add some colour before reducing, try adding in a mixture of frozen vegetables (peas, sweetcorn, green beans) or, for a slightly more filling variation, add a glass of red wine and chopped ham and/or mushrooms to the mix.

Spaghetti Bolognese

Most students have probably tried preparing this classic Italian dish at some point. There are many variations of the recipe and this original meat version can easily be adapted for vegans.

Serves 4

INGREDIENTS

1 onion

2 cloves of garlic

2 tbsp of olive oil

500 g of minced beef

1 tin of chopped tomatoes

1 carrot

2 rashers of bacon

1 large glass of red wine (optional)

1 tbsp of tomato purée

375 ml of beef or vegetable stock

Salt

Pepper

200 g of spaghetti or other pasta

Peel and chop the onion and garlic and fry gently in the oil in a large saucepan for 5 minutes, being careful not to burn them. Add the minced beef and continue frying for a further 10 minutes. Cut the bacon into small pieces and grate the carrot, and add these along with the other remaining ingredients (except the pasta).

While your sauce is reducing, which takes around 20 minutes, cook a pasta of your choice – it doesn't have to be spaghetti – according to packet instructions. It's up to you whether you want to pile the mixture on top of the pasta on a plate or combine the two, but either way a sprinkling of Parmesan on top finishes it off perfectly.

Carbonara

This version of the classic dish is another firm favourite.

Serves 3 to 4

INGREDIENTS

200 g of pasta of your
choice

1 clove of garlic

6 rashers of streaky
bacon

2 tbsp of olive oil

50 g of Parmesan
cheese

3 egg yolks, beaten

3 tbsp single cream

Salt

Pepper

Boil the pasta according to the instructions on the packet. Five minutes before the pasta is cooked, peel and chop the garlic and cut the bacon into small pieces and fry in olive oil for 4 to 5 minutes. When the pasta is cooked, drain, and add to the bacon. Then grate the cheese, and add to the pan with the yolks, cream and seasoning. Heat until the egg has cooked, stirring constantly (this should take just a couple of minutes), then serve immediately with more pepper.

Parsley Pasta

This sounds very simple, but the taste is wonderful on its own – don't be tempted to try to make it more exciting!

Serves 2

INGREDIENTS

100 g of wholemeal pasta shells
25 g of butter
25 or 50 g of Cheddar cheese
3 tbsp of fresh flat-leaf parsley
Salt
Pepper

Cook the pasta according to the instructions on the packet, then drain. Add the butter and allow it to melt. Grate the cheese and roughly chop the parsley and toss in with the salt and pepper until evenly distributed, then serve immediately.

Aubergine Bake

Packed full of natural goodness and bursting with flavour, this is the epitome of Italian cooking.

Serves 4

INGREDIENTS

1 large aubergine

2 onions

2 cloves of garlic

2 tbsp of olive oil

1 tin of tomatoes

1 tbsp of tomato purée

1 tsp of dried oregano

Salt

Pepper

125-g pot of natural yogurt

25 g of white breadcrumbs

75 g of Cheddar cheese

Prepare the veg: thinly slice the aubergine and peel and chop the onions and garlic. Heat the oil in a frying pan. Cook the aubergine in batches so that the slices aren't overlapping in the pan: fry until it has softened and slightly browned, then place on kitchen paper to absorb the oil. After cooking all the aubergine, use the same pan to fry the onion and garlic for 5 minutes.

The next stage is to add the tomatoes, tomato purée, oregano and seasoning to the pan. Bring to the boil, then simmer for 10 minutes before stirring in the yogurt.

Using a greased ovenproof dish, arrange the aubergine then the tomato sauce in alternate layers. Continue this until the top layer is aubergine. Cover the top with breadcrumbs and grated cheese. Bake at Gas Mark 4 (180°C, 350°F) for 30 minutes.

Serve with rice or potatoes.

Lasagne

An Italian classic, loved by many. Always a winner.

Serves 4

INGREDIENTS

1 large onion

2 cloves of garlic

2 tbsp of olive oil

500 g of minced beef

1 tin of chopped
  tomatoes

2 tsp of oregano

125 ml of beef stock

2 tbsp of tomato purée

Salt

Pepper

1 packet of lasagne
  ("no pre-cooking
  required" type)

For the cheese sauce:

25 g of butter

50 g of flour

500 ml of milk

150 g of cheese, grated

Peel and chop the onion and garlic and cook with the oil in a saucepan for 5 minutes. Add the mince and cook thoroughly until brown. Then add the tomatoes, oregano, stock, tomato purée and seasoning. After bringing to the boil, an optional simmering for 15 to 20 minutes will improve the flavour.

While the mince sauce is reducing, prepare the cheese sauce. Melt the butter in a saucepan and then add the flour, stirring constantly. Remove from the heat and add the milk in stages. If the milk is added in one go, you end up with lumps in the sauce. After adding the milk, bring to the boil and add the cheese, saving a bit for the top. Then simmer for 3 or 4 minutes; the sauce should now begin to thicken.

Find a shallow baking dish and grease it, then add a layer of mince sauce followed by a layer of lasagne, followed by a layer of cheese sauce. Continue this formation until you have used up your mixtures, making sure you finish with the cheese sauce. Sprinkle some cheese on top.

Bake on the middle shelf of a preheated oven at Gas Mark 6 (200°C, 400°F) for 30 to 40 minutes, until golden brown.

Pizza

Ah pizza, a staple food among students. The takeaway option may be tempting, but making your own is fun, easy and cheaper. There is huge scope for variety, both in toppings and bases, so don't be afraid to experiment! The easiest to make is the French bread pizza, because the base is simply a sliced baguette. Dough bases can be bought ready-made, but they cost more. You could experiment with other loaves, like ciabatta or sourdough, if that's more your thing.

Pizza Margherita

*This is the basic pizza. If you want to design your own,
use this and add your own toppings.*

Serves 1

INGREDIENTS

1 stick of French bread
2 tbsp tomato purée
50 g of mozzarella cheese
Pepper
Pinch of oregano
1 tsp of olive oil

Slice the French stick in half and spread some tomato
purée on top. A thin layer will do – if you put too much
on, your pizza will become soggy. Place slices of the cheese
on top, season, add the oregano (and basil if desired) and
pour on the oil. Bake in the oven until the cheese turns a
golden brown colour. It should take roughly 15 minutes at
Gas Mark 7 (220°C, 425°F).

Pizza Roma

The tuna and onion create a wonderful a-Roma in this Italian classic!

Serves 1

INGREDIENTS

1 stick of French bread
2 tbsp tomato purée
50 g of tinned tuna
2 to 3 onion rings
25 g of cheese, grated
Pepper
Pinch of oregano
1 tsp of olive oil

Slice the French stick in half and spread some tomato purée on top. Scatter the tuna on top first, then the onion rings and finally the cheese. Season, add the oregano and oil and cook as for the previous recipe.

Other Variations

There is almost no limit to what you can put on a pizza. Here is a list of suggested toppings that can be used as a basis for designing your own.

- Anchovies
- Capers
- Egg
- Exotic cheeses
- Fresh tomatoes
- Green peppers
- Ham
- Hot green chilli peppers
- Leeks

- Mushrooms
- Olives
- Onions
- Pepperoni
- Pineapple
- Red peppers
- Spinach
- Sweetcorn
- Tuna

Coq au Vin

This legendary recipe is perfect on a cold winter's evening.

Serves 4

INGREDIENTS

50 g of butter

1.5 kg of chicken

10 shallots

1 clove of garlic

225 g of small
   mushrooms

100 g of streaky bacon

300 ml of red wine

150 ml of chicken stock

1 bay leaf

Salt

Pepper

1 tbsp of fresh parsley

For the beurre manié:

2 tbsp flour

2 tbsp butter

Melt the butter in a large casserole dish, then cut the chicken into pieces and fry for 5 minutes until golden brown. Remove from the dish and set aside.

Peel and chop the shallots and garlic, chop the mushrooms and cut the bacon into strips, then fry for 5 minutes. Now add the chicken pieces.

Pour in the red wine and stock, and add the bay leaf and seasoning, then bring to the boil. Simmer for about 2 hours.

While the chicken is simmering, prepare the *beurre manié* (which is French for "kneaded butter") by mixing the flour and the butter together to form a soft paste. Split the *beurre manié* into acorn-sized pieces and drop into the sauce in your casserole dish, stirring constantly to avoid any lumps.

Remove the bay leaf before serving and garnish with the chopped parsley.

Chicken in Beer

The temptation is always to leave out the chicken from this recipe.

Serves 4

INGREDIENTS

1 onion
2 tbsp of olive oil
4 chicken pieces
3 carrots
1 leek

100 g of mushrooms
1 large can of your
   favourite lager/ale
Salt
Pepper

Peel and chop the onion, then fry in the oil in a casserole dish for 3 to 4 minutes. Add the chicken and fry for another 10 minutes. Slice the carrots, leek and mushrooms and chuck them in the dish along with the lager/ale and seasoning, then stick in the oven for 1 hour at Gas Mark 5 (190°C, 375°F). Then finish off your four-pack of beer.

Lemon Chicken

A refreshing and zesty twist on a simple chicken dish.

Serves 2

INGREDIENTS

2 chicken breasts
2 tbsp of olive oil
Juice of 1 lemon
Salt
Pepper

Cut the chicken into small pieces (this allows the lemon flavour to infuse more fully). Heat the oil in a large frying pan, then add the chicken, lemon juice and seasoning. Fry for 5 minutes, or until the chicken is cooked all the way through, adding more lemon juice before serving if required. Serve with a salad and pitta or French bread.

Pork Provençal

This classic French dish is simple to prepare and brings out the best in cheaper cuts of meat.

Serves 4

INGREDIENTS

1 onion

1 clove of garlic

2 tbsp of olive oil

1 tin of chopped tomatoes

1 red pepper

1 courgette

2 tsp of herbes de Provence or mixed herbs

Salt

Pepper

4 pork chops

4 slices of Cheddar cheese

Peel and chop the onion and garlic, then fry in the oil in a saucepan for about 5 minutes. When these have cooked, add the tomatoes, chopped red pepper and courgette, herbs and seasoning. Let the sauce simmer for 20 minutes.

After 10 minutes, grill the pork on foil to catch the fat, turning occasionally, and when it is nearly cooked put some sauce and the slices of cheese on the pork and grill until the cheese begins to melt.

Note that thinner pork chops will take less cooking time.

Serve with potatoes and fresh vegetables and the rest of the sauce.

Ratatouille

This traditional Provençal recipe can really be made from whatever seasonal vegetables are available.

Serves 4

INGREDIENTS

1 small aubergine

2 onions

2 cloves of garlic

1 courgette

1 lemon (optional)

1 red pepper

2 tbsp of olive oil

1 tin of chopped tomatoes

2 tsp of rosemary

1 bay leaf

1 glass of red wine, water or tomato juice (optional)

Salt

Pepper

Before you prepare the other vegetables, slice the aubergine and place the pieces on a plate, and lightly sprinkle them with salt. Leave for an hour. Then peel and finely chop the onions and garlic, thinly slice the courgette, quarter the lemon, and deseed and chop the red pepper.

Now wash the aubergine pieces to remove the salt, then dry them with kitchen paper, and dice. Heat the oil in a large saucepan. Fry the onions and garlic for about 5 minutes, then add the courgette, aubergine and pepper. Cook for about 5 minutes, then add the tomatoes, lemon and other ingredients. Bring to the boil and then simmer for 20 minutes.

Ratatouille can be served with almost anything – rice, baked potato, pitta bread, etc. It can also be served cold.

Vegetable Stir-fry

Your basic stir-fry – healthy, tasty and surprisingly filling.

Serves 4

INGREDIENTS

1 onion
1 clove of garlic
1 carrot
1 red pepper
1 green pepper
2 tbsp of olive oil
1 tin of water chestnuts (optional)
1 tin of bamboo shoots
2 tbsp of soy sauce
Salt
Pepper
1 pack of fresh beansprouts

Prepare all the vegetables first: peel and chop the onion, garlic and carrot, and chop and deseed the red and green peppers. Pour the oil into your wok or frying pan over a high heat, then when it is smoking (try not to set fire to the kitchen in the process), add the onion and garlic, and fry for 5 minutes, stirring constantly to avoid burning.

If you are using water chestnuts, cook these next as they take the longest to cook, and are nicer when they are slightly crispy. Then add the soy sauce, seasoning and other vegetables except for the beansprouts.

After frying the vegetables for about 5 to 10 minutes, add the beansprouts and cook for a couple more minutes. It is important to keep the beansprouts firm.

Serve with rice or noodles.

Pork Stir-Fry

The pork really lifts the flavour of this dish, but you could try using other meats or a meat-free alternative – just make sure it's cooked right through.

Serves 2

INGREDIENTS

2 tbsp of olive oil
250 g of diced pork
1 green pepper, deseeded and chopped
1 onion, peeled and chopped
2 tsp of chilli powder
1 clove of garlic, peeled and sliced
1 tbsp of soy sauce

Heat the oil in a large frying pan or wok, then fry the onion and the garlic for about 3 to 4 minutes.

Add the pepper, soy sauce, chilli powder and the pork and fry until the pork is cooked. This should take about 10 minutes, depending on the size of the meat pieces.

Serve with rice.

Thai Fish Cakes

This is a jazzed-up version of the fish cakes your mum used to make – always a sure-fire winner.

Serves 2

INGREDIENTS

4 spring onions
2 tbsp of fresh coriander
500 g of white fish, such as cod or haddock
2 tsp of Thai red curry paste
1 tsp of fish sauce
1 tsp of lime juice
Salt
Pepper
2 tbsp of vegetable oil

Chop the spring onions and fresh coriander, then place all the ingredients into a food processor, except the oil, and give a quick blitz. Don't overdo it so it ends up being a purée. Remove the mixture and shape into small patties. You should be able to make about 12 small fish cakes.

Heat the oil in a frying pan and fry the fish cakes in batches until golden brown.

Serve with salad and Thai dipping sauce.

Teriyaki Salmon

The taste of salmon alone is enough to make most
people drool, but add teriyaki and ginger and you get
a gloriously tasty dish every time.

Serves 2

INGREDIENTS

3 tsp of fresh ginger
4 tbsp of teriyaki sauce
1 tsp of sugar
1 tbsp of water
1 tsp of sesame oil
2 salmon fillets

To create the marinade, peel and grate the ginger, then combine with the teriyaki sauce, sugar, water and oil in a bowl big enough to hold the salmon fillets. Place the salmon fillets in the marinade and leave for 30 minutes.

Remove the salmon from the marinade and place on tin foil and grill for approximately 10 minutes, depending on the thickness of the fillets.

This is delicious served with steamed pak choi.

Red Thai Curry

The intense flavours of this dish have made it a classic the world over.

Serves 4

INGREDIENTS

1 tbsp of ground nut oil

1 tbsp of red Thai curry paste

3 chicken breasts

1 400-ml tin of coconut milk

1 cup of water

1 red pepper

2 tsp of brown sugar

2 tsp of grated lime rind

1 tbsp of fish sauce

Heat the oil in a wok or large frying pan on a high heat. Add the curry paste and cook for a minute, stirring as it cooks. Don't let it burn.

Cut the chicken into chunks and stir-fry for 3 to 4 minutes until browned, after which add the coconut milk and water. Bring to the boil, then chop and deseed the red pepper and add to the wok, then simmer for 10 minutes.

Finally, add the sugar, lime and fish sauce and cook gently for a further 5 minutes.

Serve with rice.

Vegetable Curry

There are literally thousands of different recipes for curry, but a vegetable curry is both amazingly cheap and suitable for freezing.

Serves 4

INGREDIENTS

1 onion

2 cloves of garlic

2 tbsp of olive oil

1 tbsp of Madras curry powder

4 potatoes

2 courgettes

1 leek

1 tin of chopped tomatoes

1 dried red chilli

250 ml of vegetable stock

Any spare vegetables

1 to 2 tbsp of water

Salt

Pepper

1 small pot of natural yogurt

Peel and chop the onion and garlic, then fry in the oil in a large saucepan with the curry powder for 5 minutes or until the onion has softened.

Dice the potatoes into 2.5-cm (1-inch) cubes, and slice the courgettes and leek. Add these to the pan, along with all the other ingredients except the yogurt. Season, then bring to the boil, and simmer for 40 minutes or more. Add the yogurt 5 minutes before serving.

While the curry is simmering, taste it to see if it is to the strength required. If it is not hot enough, just add more curry powder. Serve with rice – use basmati rice for the best flavour, though any long-grain rice will be fine.

Chicken Curry

You can't go wrong with this absolute classic.

Serves 4

INGREDIENTS

2 onions

2 cloves of garlic

2 tbsp of olive oil

3 tsp of curry powder

1 tsp of garam masala

2 fresh green chilli peppers

4 chicken pieces

1 to 2 tbsp of water

Salt

Pepper

1 tin of chopped tomatoes

3 whole green cardamom pods

2 tbsp of coriander

1 small pot of natural yogurt

Peel and chop the onions and garlic and fry in the oil in a large saucepan for 5 minutes or until they have softened.

Add the curry powder, garam masala and chillies, chopped into rings, and fry for a couple more minutes. Add the chicken and water and fry for 5 minutes. Season. Add the chopped tomatoes, cardamom pods and chopped coriander. Simmer for 30 to 40 minutes.

Add the yogurt about 5 minutes before serving. Serve with basmati rice.

Goulash

This Hungarian dish traditionally uses veal, but beef makes a very good substitute.

Serves 4

INGREDIENTS

2 tbsp of olive oil

1 large onion

1 clove of garlic

500 g of stewing beef

1 red pepper

1 green pepper

2 carrots

1 parsnip

1 tin of chopped tomatoes

1 tbsp of paprika

½ tsp of caraway seeds

1 tsp of mixed herbs

Salt

Pepper

375 ml of beef stock

500 g of potatoes

125 ml of sour cream (optional)

Peel and chop the onion and garlic and fry with the oil for a couple of minutes in a casserole dish or a large saucepan.

Cut the meat into bite-size cubes, deseed and chop the peppers, and dice the carrots and parsnip. Add these to the dish along with the tomatoes, paprika, caraway seeds, herbs, salt and pepper, and cook for about 5 minutes.

Add the stock and simmer for about 40 minutes. Peel and slice the potatoes and add them to the dish, cooking for a further 30 minutes. Then stir in the sour cream, if desired, and serve.

Chilli Con Carne

Chilli can be as hot as desired, but remember that even though you may love to sweat, your housemates might prefer it a little milder.

Serves 4

INGREDIENTS

1 large onion

2 cloves of garlic

2 tbsp of olive oil

3 tsp of chilli powder

500 g of minced beef

1 or 2 red/green chilli
  peppers

1 tin of chopped
  tomatoes

1 tsp of oregano

1 tbsp of tomato purée

Salt

Pepper

125 ml of beef stock

1 glass of red wine
  (optional)

1 tin of kidney beans

Peel and finely chop the onion and garlic, and fry in the oil with the chilli powder for about 5 minutes. Add the mince, and cook for about 10 minutes, stirring constantly to stop it burning.

Add the other ingredients, except the kidney beans, varying the amounts of seasoning according to taste. Bring to the boil, then simmer for about 20 minutes (the longer the better).

Drain the kidney beans and add them to the pan 5 minutes before serving.

Serve with rice, pitta bread or jacket potatoes.

Paella

This is probably Spain's most well-known dish. To make this dish suitable for non-meat eaters, just replace the seafood and chicken with plenty of extra veggies, and remember to swap the chicken stock for vegetable.

Serves 4 to 5

INGREDIENTS

2 onions
2 cloves of garlic
4 tbsp of olive oil
Salt
Pepper
200 g of rice
4 tomatoes
Pinch of saffron

500 ml of chicken stock
4 chicken pieces
1 green pepper
100 g of frozen peas
100 g of cooked mussels (optional)
100 g of peeled prawns (optional)

Peel and chop the onions and garlic, and fry in half of the oil in a large frying pan, or preferably a wok, for 3 to 4 minutes. Season. Remove the seeds from the tomatoes (cut in half from side to side – not top to bottom – and squeeze gently until the seeds have all come out). Add the rice, saffron, tomatoes and stock, bring to the boil, then cook gently for 10 minutes.

Fry the chicken in a separate pan with the remaining oil for 10 minutes or until lightly browned. Then add the chicken to the rice, deseed and chop the green pepper and stir in with the other ingredients, and simmer until the rice is cooked (this can take up to another 30 minutes, but keep tasting the rice throughout cooking to check).

Serve with lemon wedges.

Piperade

This pepper-based dish is quick and easy to prepare and is suitable for a light lunch or dinner. It originates from the Basque Country. Add a pinch of paprika if you want it with a little bite, or ham if you want to bulk it up.

Serves 4

INGREDIENTS

2 red peppers

2 green peppers

6 tomatoes

2 cloves of garlic

1 tbsp of fresh basil

2 tbsp of butter

Salt

Pepper

6 eggs

Cut the peppers into strips and deseed them, and skin and chop the tomatoes (you could use tinned tomatoes, although it won't have the same consistency). Peel and chop the garlic, and chop the basil.

Heat the butter in a frying pan and cook the peppers for 10 minutes. Add the tomatoes, garlic, basil and seasoning and cook until the tomatoes are almost a pulp. Take care that the vegetables do not burn.

While the vegetables are cooking, beat the eggs in a basin. When the vegetables are ready add the eggs. Stir the mixture until it thickens, but do not let the eggs set completely.

Avocado Salad

The luxurious taste of avocados can turn an ordinary salad into something truly indulgent. This superfood is bursting with healthy vitamins and minerals, making it a perfect pick-me-up after a heavy weekend. When choosing an avocado to be eaten straight away make sure it is ripe – it should be slightly soft when the skin is pressed.

INGREDIENTS

1 avocado
6 cherry tomatoes
½ a red onion
French or balsamic dressing

Remove the skin of the avocado using a knife. Then cut in half lengthways, around the stone in the middle and pull the two halves away from each other. The stone will stay lodged in one side. The easiest way of removing the stone is to carefully press the blade of a sharp knife in it and then ease it out.

After removing the stone, cut the avocado into slices. Cut the cherry tomatoes in half, and peel and finely slice the red onion into rings. Toss together and cover with the dressing. You could try variations of this salad by adding salad leaves, couscous, cooked bacon or mango.

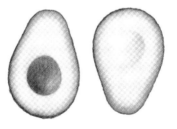

Salade Niçoise

There has long been a raging debate over what makes the perfect niçoise: tuna or anchovies? Olives or green beans? We say, throw it all in! This recipe traditionally uses tuna steak, but you get the same taste from a tin and for a fraction of the price.

Serves 4

INGREDIENTS

2 eggs
150 g of French beans
1 lettuce
3 tomatoes
200-g tin of tuna

French dressing
10 black olives
6 anchovy fillets (optional)
Salt
Pepper

Hard-boil the eggs for 8 minutes, adding the beans for the last few minutes to cook them through, then place the eggs in a bowl of cold water. Wash the lettuce and place the leaves in a large serving bowl, then add the tuna (drain the oil first) and toss it all together.

Quarter the tomatoes and place them on top of the lettuce. Shell the eggs, cut them into quarters, and arrange them neatly on top. Pour the dressing over the salad and add the olives, beans and anchovies, if desired. Season and serve.

Italian Pepper Salad

There are many ways of serving peppers but this simple recipe is one of the best.

Serves 4

INGREDIENTS

4 large peppers (mixture of colours)
1 tsp of capers
4 tbsp of olive oil
Salt
Pepper

Preheat the oven to the highest setting possible, and place the whole peppers on a tray on the top shelf. Roast for 20 to 30 minutes, turning halfway through so they are evenly cooked.

Remove from the oven and put the peppers in a clean polythene bag and tie closed, or use any airtight container – this helps to "steam" them and loosen the skin. Leave the peppers sealed in there for at least 15 minutes before removing them to peel off the skins. Make sure all the skin is removed, as when it is burnt it has a very strong flavour and can taint the dish.

Next remove the stems and seeds and cut into strips. Place the sliced peppers in a serving dish with the capers, drizzle with the oil and then season. There will normally be some residue from the peppers in the polythene bag that can be added to the dish for extra flavour. To add extra healthy goodness, try serving it on a large bed of salad leaves.

Tomato and Onion Salad

A typical Provençal salad – and a classic combination of flavours.

Serves 4

INGREDIENTS

1 red onion	**Salt**
4 fresh tomatoes	**Pepper**
Fresh basil	**French dressing**

Peel the onion and slice fairly thinly. Slice the tomatoes and arrange them on a large plate or dish. Place the onion pieces between the tomato slices. Decorate with the basil leaves, and season well. Pour the French dressing over the top.

SNACKS AND MIDNIGHT CRAVINGS

Omelette

A really easy way to use up eggs, or knock together a quick and filling snack.

Serves 1 to 2

INGREDIENTS

2 or 3 eggs
Pinch of mixed herbs
Salt
Pepper
25 g of butter

Beat the eggs together in a mixing bowl and add the seasoning. Melt the butter in a frying pan on a medium heat and pour in the eggs.

As soon as the eggs start to cook, lift up one edge of the omelette with a spatula, tilt the pan and let the uncooked egg run underneath. Continue to do this until the omelette is cooked, then flip it in half and serve on a warmed plate.

To add interest, you could try one of these variations:

Cheese and Tomato

Prepare as above, but add 50 g of grated cheese and 1 chopped tomato before pouring into the frying pan.

Bacon

Cut 2 rashers of bacon up into little pieces and fry for a couple of minutes, then add to the mixture and follow the instructions above.

Welsh Rarebit

Doesn't taste particularly Welsh, nor is it very rare.
But there's no doubt that it's delicious.

Serves 1

INGREDIENTS

150 g of Cheddar cheese
15 g of butter
½ tsp of dry mustard
2 tbsp of flour
2 slices of bread

Grate the cheese and put into a small saucepan. Add the butter and mustard, then cook gently, stirring constantly, until the cheese has melted. Take the saucepan away from the heat and add the flour, beating it in until smooth. Allow to cool.

Grill the bread slices (keeping an eye on them to make sure they don't burn), then spread the cheese mixture evenly over the toast. Grill until golden, then serve.

For a more traditional rarebit, you could add ale (or cider) when melting the cheese, and spread the toast with Worcestershire sauce before spreading the cheese mixture on top.

Potato, Bacon and Onion Rösti

These patties are a slightly more creative way to prepare bacon than the BLT, but they're just as mouth-watering.

Serves 4

INGREDIENTS

1 onion
500 g of potatoes
4 rashers of bacon
2 eggs, beaten
1 tbsp of plain flour
Salt
Pepper
2 tbsp of vegetable oil

Peel the onion and potatoes, then coarsely grate them and place in a mixing bowl.

Chop the bacon into small pieces and add to the bowl, along with the eggs and flour. Mix together, then season. Heat the oil in a frying pan, then add heaped tablespoons of the mixture into the pan to form small circles.

Fry the potato cakes on both sides till they turn a golden brown. Continue doing this until all the mixture is used up.

Serve with baked beans or a salad.

Garlic Pasta

A perfect dish to repel a hunger attack, and it only takes a few minutes to prepare.

Serves 1

INGREDIENTS

100 g of pasta
2 tbsp of olive oil
½ clove of garlic

Salt
Pepper

Cook the pasta according to the instructions on the packet. When the pasta is cooked, drain and place in a small serving bowl. Using the saucepan you cooked the pasta in, heat the oil, peel and finely chop the garlic, and fry gently for a minute. Pour the oil over the pasta and mix. Season. If you wish to make it a little more exciting, add some grated cheese on top or, when frying, stir in a finely chopped small red chilli, but remove the seeds first if you don't want it too hot.

BREAKFAST RECIPES AND SMOOTHIES

Eggs

Eggs are a great source of protein, amino acids and vitamin D, plus they taste great however you prepare them.

Scrambled

Serves 2

INGREDIENTS

3 eggs
4 tbsp of milk
Pepper
25 g of butter

Whisk the eggs in a bowl and add the milk and pepper. Melt the butter in a saucepan and add the egg mixture. Stir the mixture continuously as it thickens. Don't have the heat up too high, or else the egg will burn and stick to the pan. Serve on top of hot, buttered toast.

Poached

INGREDIENTS

1 egg per person (or more if desired)

The traditional way of poaching an egg is to boil some water in a saucepan and then, after breaking the egg into a cup or mug, slide it gently into the water. Only put one egg in at a time, and wait for it to firm up before removing with a slotted spoon.

Boiled

INGREDIENTS

1 egg per person (or more if desired)
1 slice of bread per person

Boil some water in a saucepan and carefully lower the egg, whole, into the water, using a spoon. Boil the egg for 3 to 4 minutes, depending on how runny you want the yolk.

After removing the egg from the water, whack the top with a spoon – this will stop the egg from hardening. Meanwhile, toast a slice of bread and cut into long thin strips. Dunk them into the runny egg and enjoy! If you require the egg to be hard-boiled, cook for about 8 minutes in boiling water. If your egg cracks while it is cooking, pouring a tablespoon of vinegar in the water will help seal it.

Fried

Perfect with sausages and hash browns.

INGREDIENTS

1 egg per person (or more if desired)
2 tbsp of oil

Heat some oil in a frying pan, but don't let the fat get too hot or the egg will stick to the pan and bubble. Crack the egg on the side of the pan and plop the egg into the oil. Fry gently for about 3 minutes, basting occasionally and lifting the edges with a spatula as it cooks to prevent sticking. If you like your eggs American-style (over-easy), fry both sides of the egg.

French Toast

This is a wonderfully indulgent and versatile recipe. Try topping it with sliced bananas, chocolate sauce, maple syrup or strawberry jam.

Serves 2

INGREDIENTS

4 eggs
1 cup of milk
1 tsp of sugar
1 tsp of salt

Butter
Slices of bread without the crusts

Beat the eggs and the milk together and add the sugar and salt. Heat a knob of butter in a frying pan. Dip a slice of bread in the egg mixture and then heat slowly for a couple of minutes on each side until golden brown. Serve hot with your choice of toppings.

Smoothies

For those of you who can't quite manage food at breakfast time or are in need of a quick, healthy energy boost, here's a selection of delicious smoothies. You will need a blender or smoothie maker for these recipes.

Breakfast Smoothie

This is wonderfully filling and tastes so good you won't realize how healthy it actually is.

INGREDIENTS

1 large banana
200 ml of milk
2 tbsp of rolled
  porridge oats

2 tsp of runny honey
2 ice cubes

Place all of the ingredients into the blender and blend until smooth.

Mango, Strawberry and Banana Smoothie

Try adding a sprinkling of rolled oats or muesli on top to make this a more substantial breakfast.

INGREDIENTS

5 strawberries
100 g of mango flesh
1 small banana
200 ml of apple juice

Wash the strawberries carefully and cut off the green leafy tops. Chop the mango flesh. Peel and roughly chop the banana. Place all of the ingredients into the blender and blend until smooth.

Kiwi and Melon Smoothie

Zingy and sweet, super-healthy and refreshing – the perfect smoothie!

INGREDIENTS

½ honeydew melon
1 kiwi fruit
1 apple
2 tsp of honey
4 ice cubes

Peel and slice the melon and kiwi fruit. Peel the apple and core it, then cut into small chunks. Place all of the ingredients into the blender and blend until smooth.

SWEET TREATS AND DESSERTS

Chocolate Brownies

There's nothing more mouth-watering than warm chocolate brownies with a big scoop of real vanilla ice cream.

INGREDIENTS

150 g of unsalted butter
200 g of dark chocolate
2 eggs
200 g of dark muscovado sugar
100 g of plain flour
1 tsp of baking powder

Grease an 18-cm (7-inch) square cake tin with a little of the butter and line with non-stick baking parchment (or greaseproof paper).

Break the chocolate into pieces and place with the butter in a heatproof bowl over a pan of simmering water. Don't let the water boil as it will spill over.

Stir the chocolate and butter mixture together with a spoon. Beat the eggs and sugar together in a separate bowl using a handheld mixer if you have one, or by hand if you don't. Add in the melted chocolate and butter, and then the flour and baking powder. Stir thoroughly.

Pour the mixture into the tin and bake for 30 minutes, at Gas Mark 3 (160°C, 325°F). Allow to cool for 10 minutes before cutting into squares.

Low-Fat Banana Muffins

Not all cakes have to be sugar-laden and fatty – these tasty treats will make you feel that eating cake can actually be good for you.

INGREDIENTS

125 g of plain flour

50 g of light brown sugar

½ tsp of bicarbonate of soda

1 tsp of baking powder

½ tsp of ground cinnamon

100 g of rolled oats

2 eggs

2 tbsp of vegetable oil

3 medium bananas

125 ml of buttermilk

Prepare a 12-hole muffin tin with either paper liners or a thin coating of oil. Place the flour, sugar, bicarbonate, baking powder, cinnamon and oats into a large bowl and mix well.

In another bowl, beat the eggs, then add the oil. Mash the bananas and add, along with the buttermilk, then combine.

Fold this mixture into the flour mixture, and stir thoroughly. Divide the mixture between the muffin cups and bake for 20 minutes at Gas Mark 6 (200°C, 400°F).

Leave to cool for 10 minutes in the tin, then turn out onto a wire rack.

Flapjacks

For those with access to two baking trays and living in a large household it can be advisable to double the quantities given here, as flapjacks tend to disappear fast!

INGREDIENTS

100 g of butter
4 tbsp of golden syrup
75 g of sugar
Pinch of salt
200 g of porridge oats

Grease a shallow baking tray with a knob of butter. Melt the butter in a large saucepan, then add the syrup and leave over a low heat for a couple of minutes, stirring continuously.

Remove from the heat and add the sugar, salt and oats. Mix thoroughly using a wooden spoon, making sure all the oats are covered with syrup.

Spoon the mixture evenly into the baking try, and cook for 20 to 30 minutes at Gas Mark 4 (180°C, 350°F).

Cut the flapjacks into bars *before* they cool.

Croissant Pudding

Once you introduce this sinful treat to your friends they're bound to demand it again and again.

Serves 4

INGREDIENTS

5 croissants
Butter
2 egg yolks
50 g of caster sugar
300 ml of milk
300 ml of double cream
2 drops of vanilla essence
50 g of raisins
Ground cinnamon
Brown sugar

Cut the croissants lengthways and then in half. Butter one side of the croissants and put to one side. Beat the egg yolks, caster sugar, milk, cream and vanilla essence, then put aside. Grease an ovenproof dish with a knob of butter and place a layer of croissants on the bottom, then sprinkle with raisins. Continue layering until all the croissants are used up.

Briefly beat the milk mixture, then pour over the croissants. Sprinkle with cinnamon. Leave to soak for at least 30 minutes.

While the croissants are soaking, preheat the oven to Gas Mark 4 (180 °C, 350 °F).

Sprinkle a thin layer of brown sugar over the top of the dish. Put the dish in a deep-sided baking tray and pour boiling water into the tin, roughly halfway up the side of the cake dish, making sure it doesn't spill over into the dish. This helps the cooking process. Cook in the middle of the oven for 40 minutes.

Raspberry Brûlée

Traditionally brûlées are finished off with a kitchen blowtorch. Thankfully, this method is far safer and guaranteed to produce a perfect pud.

Serves 4

INGREDIENTS

250 g of fresh raspberries
250 ml of double cream
150 g of demerara or golden granulated sugar

Place the raspberries in a shallow heatproof dish. Whip the cream until thick (but not too stiff), and spread over the raspberries. Sprinkle the sugar over the cream, covering it completely. Place under a preheated grill until it is dark and bubbling. Remove from the grill and leave to cool, then chill in the fridge for a couple of hours. If raspberries are out of season or too pricey, an equally tasty version can be made using sliced banana.

Baked Apples

This healthy pud has stood the test of time. If you don't have mincemeat, try making your own with raisins, currants and sultanas mixed with brown sugar and plenty of cinnamon.

INGREDIENTS

1 large cooking apple per person
Mincemeat
Brown sugar
Butter

Remove the cores from the apples and stand them in an ovenproof dish. Fill the hole in each apple with mincemeat and a teaspoon of brown sugar. Add a knob of butter on top. Put enough water in the dish to cover the bottom of the apples. Bake at Gas Mark 4 (180°C, 350°F) for about an hour. Test an apple with a skewer; it should be soft, but not too soft. Serve with cream or a scoop of vanilla ice cream.

Pancakes

Pancakes make a great treat any day of the year, not just Shrove Tuesday!

Serves 4

INGREDIENTS

100 g of plain flour
Pinch of salt
1 egg
250 ml of milk
Butter or oil

Put the flour and salt in a bowl and add the egg into the middle. Pour in about a third of the milk. Stir gently, adding the rest of milk a little at a time. Beat the mixture thoroughly, then pour into a jug.

Melt a small knob of butter in a frying pan or heat a few drops of oil, then add a couple of tablespoons of the batter. Tip the frying pan to spread the mixture evenly.

Fry until the underside is brown, using a spatula to lift the edges so that they don't stick, then toss the pancake (or, if there's no one around to impress, you could flip the pancake using a spatula or palette knife).

Tip the finished pancake onto a plate. Serve with lemon juice and sugar, or maple syrup.

Fresh Fruit Salad

Not even a hint of chocolate, just a sprinkling of sugar and all your fruity favourites.

Serves 4

INGREDIENTS

1 banana
2 oranges
1 apple
1 pear
50 g of grapes
100 g of strawberries
Juice of 1 lemon
2 tbsp of sugar
150 ml of water

The above ingredients are just a guide. Wash all fruit before starting. Put the lemon juice and sugar in a bowl and mix together.

Cut the apple into quarters, remove the core and chop into small pieces. Peel the oranges and, using a sharp knife, cut into segments, cutting between the membranes and making sure all the pips are removed.

Cut the grapes in half and remove any pips. Peel the banana and cut into slices. Skin and quarter the pear, then core it and chop into small pieces. The strawberries should be hulled (remove the leafy green bit at the top), and cut in half.

Put all the fruit in the bowl with the lemon juice, sugar and water, and mix thoroughly. Serve either on its own or with cream. If you're not eating it straight away or have leftovers, store in an airtight container in the fridge, covered in the syrup.

Black Forest Coffee

This is almost a dessert in itself, very simple to make but strictly for those with a sweet tooth.

Serves 1

INGREDIENTS

150 ml of hot coffee
2 tbsp of chocolate syrup
1 tbsp of cherry juice (maraschino or morello)
Cherries (maraschino or morello)
Whipped cream
Chocolate shavings

Mix the coffee, chocolate syrup and cherry juice in a cup. Top with whipped cream, then, removing any stones from cherries (if they are fresh), sprinkle them on top along with the chocolate shavings.